ANIMALS AROUND THE WORLD

ALL ABOUT AFRICAN
RHINOS

EZ
READERS

Robert Scally

Creating Young Nonfiction Readers

EZ Readers lets children delve into nonfiction at beginning reading levels. Young readers are introduced to new concepts, facts, ideas, and vocabulary.

Tips for Reading Nonfiction with Beginning Readers

Talk about Nonfiction
Begin by explaining that nonfiction books give us information that is true. The book will be organized around a specific topic or idea, and we may learn new facts through reading.

Look at the Parts
Most nonfiction books have helpful features. Our *EZ Readers* include a Contents page, an index, and color photographs. Share the purpose of these features with your reader.

Contents
Located at the front of a book, the Contents displays a list of the big ideas within the book and where to find them.

Index
An index is an alphabetical list of topics and the page numbers where they are found.

Glossary
Located at the back of the book, a glossary contains key words/phrases that are related to the topic.

Photos/Charts
A lot of information can be found by "reading" the charts and photos found within nonfiction text. Help your reader learn more about the different ways information can be displayed.

With a little help and guidance about reading nonfiction, you can feel good about introducing a young reader to the world of *EZ Readers* nonfiction books.

3 9082 14207 1110

Mitchell Lane
PUBLISHERS

2001 SW 31st Avenue
Hallandale, FL 33009
www.mitchelllane.com

First Edition, 2020.

Author: Robert Scally
Designer: Ed Morgan
Editor: Sharon F. Doorasamy

Names/credits:
Title: All About African Rhinos / by Robert Scally
Description: Hallandale, FL : Mitchell Lane Publishers, [2020]

Series: Animals Around the World
Library bound ISBN: 9781680203912
eBook ISBN: 9781680203929

EZ readers is an imprint of Mitchell Lane Publishers

Library of Congress Cataloging-in-Publication Data
Names: Scally, Robert, 1958- author.
Title: All about the African rhinos / by Robert Scally.
Description: First edition. | Hallandale, FL :
  EZ Readers, an imprint of Mitchell Lane Publishers, 2020.
  | Series: Animals around the world-Africa animals | Includes bibliographical references and index.
Identifiers: LCCN 2018028572| ISBN 9781680203912
  (library bound) | ISBN 9781680203929 (ebook)
Subjects: LCSH: Rhinoceroses—Africa—Juvenile literature.
Classification: LCC QL737.U63 S28 2020 |
  DDC 599.66/81392—dc23
LC record available at https://lccn.loc.gov/2018028572

Photo credits: cover, Casey Allen from Pexels, Freepik.com, p. 4-5 Shripal Daphtary on Unsplash, p. 6-7 Lucas Alexander on Unsplash, p. 8-9 Matthias Mullie on Unsplash, p. 10-11 Shutterstock, p. 12-13 Shutterstock, p. 14-15 Simon Greenwood on Unsplash, p. 16-17 Shutterstock, p. 18-19 Shutterstock, p. 20-21 Shutterstock, mapchart.net

CONTENTS

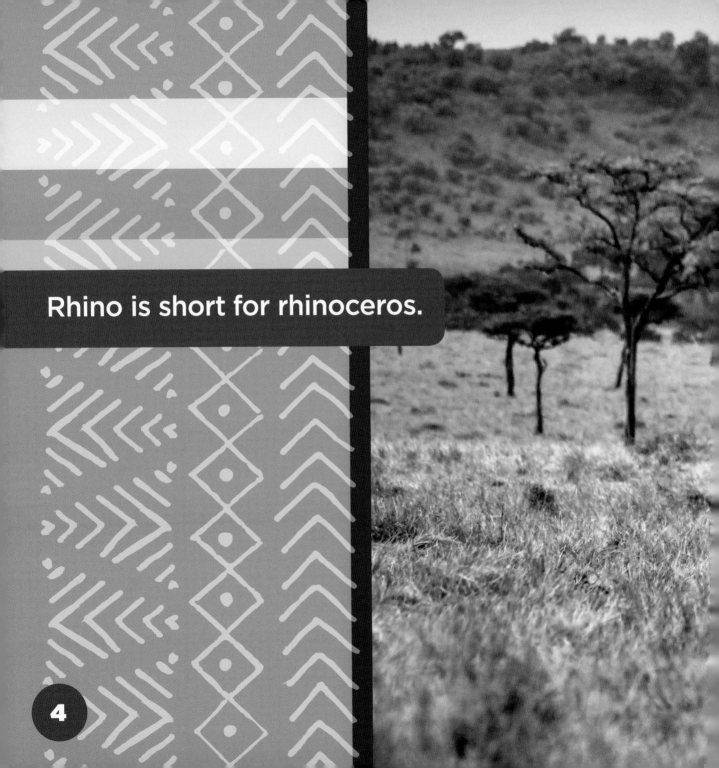

Rhino is short for rhinoceros.

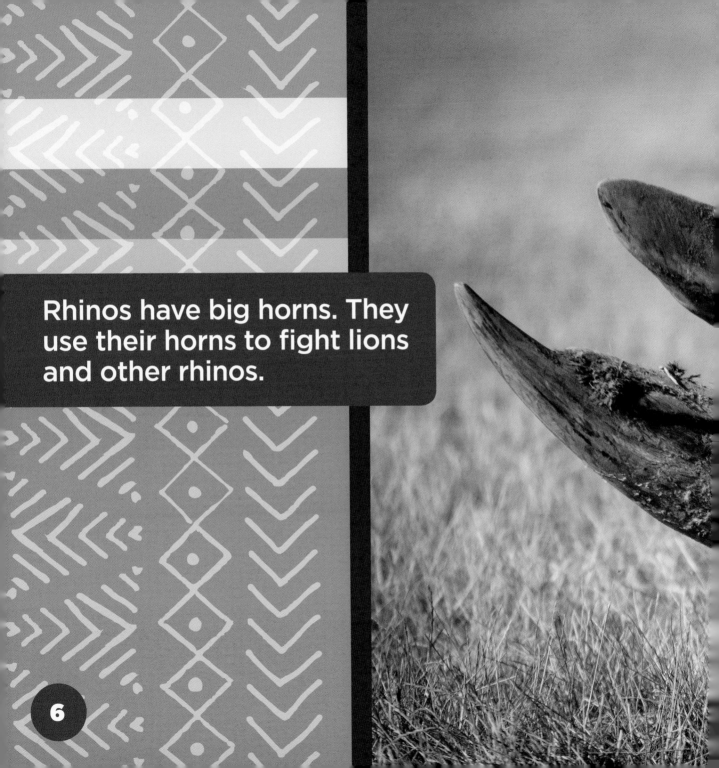

Rhinos have big horns. They use their horns to fight lions and other rhinos.

6

Rhinos live in grasslands, **savannahs**, and bush.

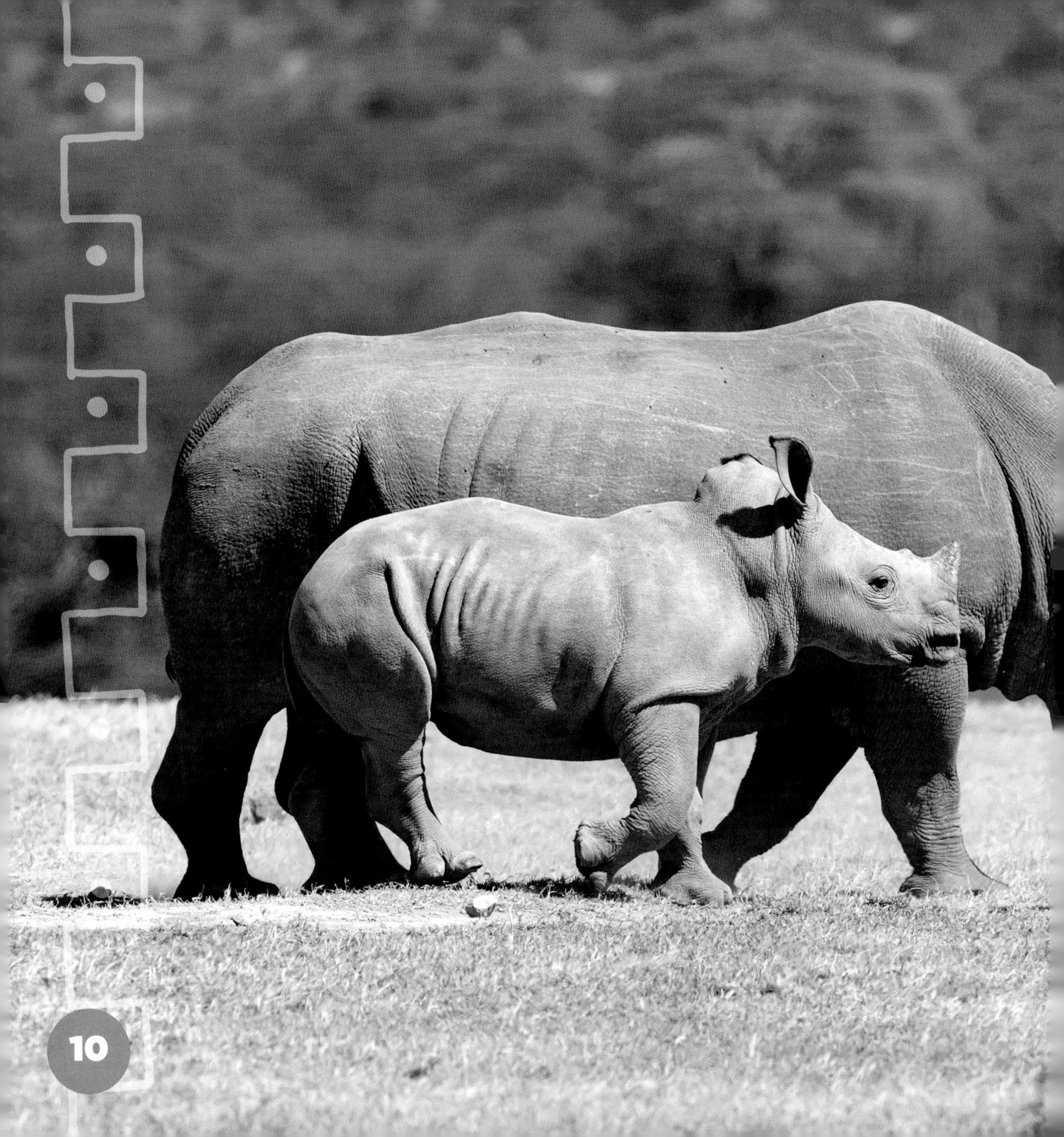

A rhino group is a **crash**.
A young rhino is a **calf**.

There are five kinds of rhinos. Black and white rhinos live in Africa. The others live in Asia.

Black rhinos are not black. White rhinos are not white. Both are gray.

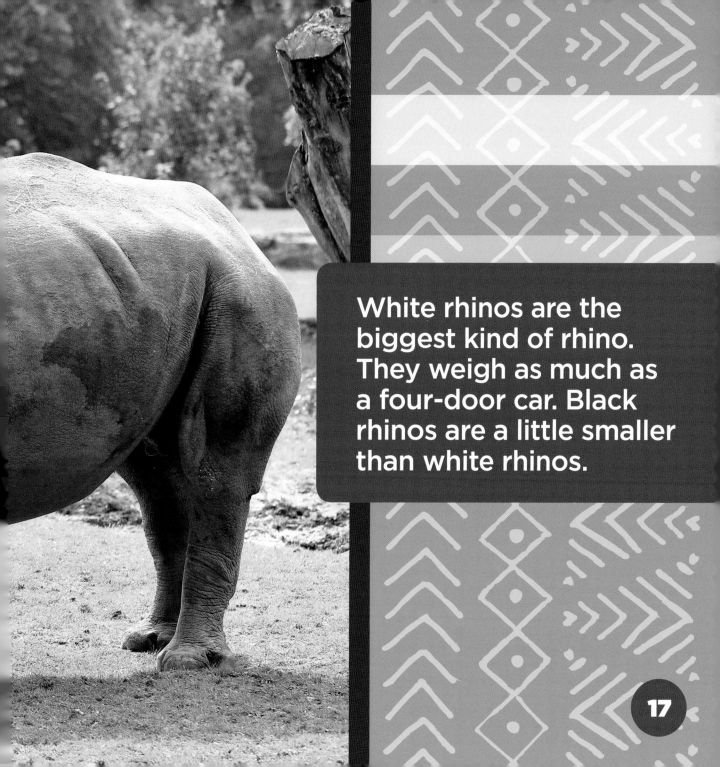

White rhinos are the biggest kind of rhino. They weigh as much as a four-door car. Black rhinos are a little smaller than white rhinos.

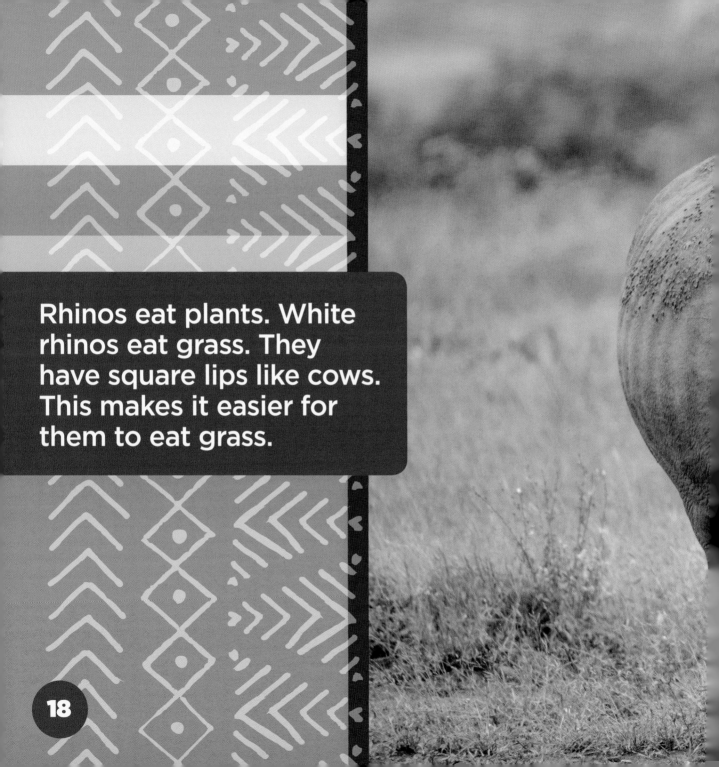

Rhinos eat plants. White rhinos eat grass. They have square lips like cows. This makes it easier for them to eat grass.

Black rhinos eat leaves. Black rhinos have pointed upper lips. They use their lips for grabbing leaves.

WHERE DO RHINOS LIVE?

Kenya
Namibia
South Africa
Zimbabwe

white and black rhinos

black rhinos

22

INTERESTING FACTS

- Rhinos are one of the largest land animals.

- Wild rhinos live 35 years.

- Rhinos can run 30 miles per hour. That is about as fast as a car on a city street.

PARTS OF A RHINO

Head
A rhino's head has a large nose with two horns.

Horns
Rhinos have two horns, one behind the other.

Lips
White rhinos have square lips for eating grass. Black rhinos have pointed lips for grabbing leaves from trees and bushes.

Skin
Rhinos have thick skin that protects them from the sun and from being scratched by branches.

GLOSSARY

crash
A group of rhinos

calf
A young rhino

savannah
A part of Africa with grass and trees

FURTHER READING

Meeker, Clare Hodgson. *National Geographic Kids Chapters: Rhino Rescue: And More True Stories of Saving Animals*. Washington, DC: National Geographic Children's Books, 2016.

Martin, M. *Rhinos: Horned Beast of the African Grasslands*. CreateSpace Independent Publishing Platform, 2014.

ON THE INTERNET

Basic Facts About Rhinoceroses. Defenders Of Wildlife
https://defenders.org/rhinoceros/basic-facts

International Rhino Foundation
https://rhinos.org/

INDEX